Colour Nature Library

HORSES

By
JANE BURTON

Designed by
DAVID GIBBON

Produced by
TED SMART

COLOUR LIBRARY BOOKS

Published 1987 by Colour Library Books Ltd,
Guildford, Surrey, England.
© 1987 Colour Library Ltd.
© Illustrations: Bruce Coleman Ltd.
Printed and bound in Barcelona, Spain by Cronion, S.A.
ISBN 0 862835 76 3

3

4

Horses and History

Horses help us to relive history. Ever since man first tamed and domesticated the wild ponies of the steppes, the horse has played an all-important role in the human saga. Not only was all agricultural labour, all land transport and all trade carried out for centuries with the help of the horse, but on the battlefield its use shaped the course of history. Today, the internal combustion engine has almost entirely eliminated man's dependence on horse-power, both everyday and in wartime; yet the horse has not bowed out before superior competition. Its role has simply changed, from slave to partner.

It is not known where, when or by whom the horse was first domesticated. Men of the Stone Age hunted wild horses for food, and most likely first herded them like cattle for meat, milk and hides long before learning to ride and harness them. Probably, the first horsemen were the barbarian nomads of central Asia who tamed and rode hardy wild ponies about four thousand years ago and later introduced them to the civilized peoples of the ancient world. But wherever and whenever the horse was first ridden, by the end of the Bronze Age about a thousand years later its potential in human warfare had been realised. At first horses were deployed on the field of battle to draw chariots, providing a new mobility and striking force which revolutionised the art of warfare.

For another thousand years chariotry became the most important feature of armies, consolidating and extending or breaking up and annihilating civilisations. Then, around the beginning of the Christian era, missile weapons such as the javelin and bow began to replace hand-to-hand sword fighting, to the fatal disadvantage of the unprotected charioteers. Armies had therefore to rethink the use of their horses, and began to redeploy them as chargers. From then on, for nearly another two millenia, the major force in battle was cavalry. At first the mounted soldiers were lightly armed, on light, fast horses;

Previous page. Japanese horses.

Right. A member of the Royal Regiment of Horse Guards.

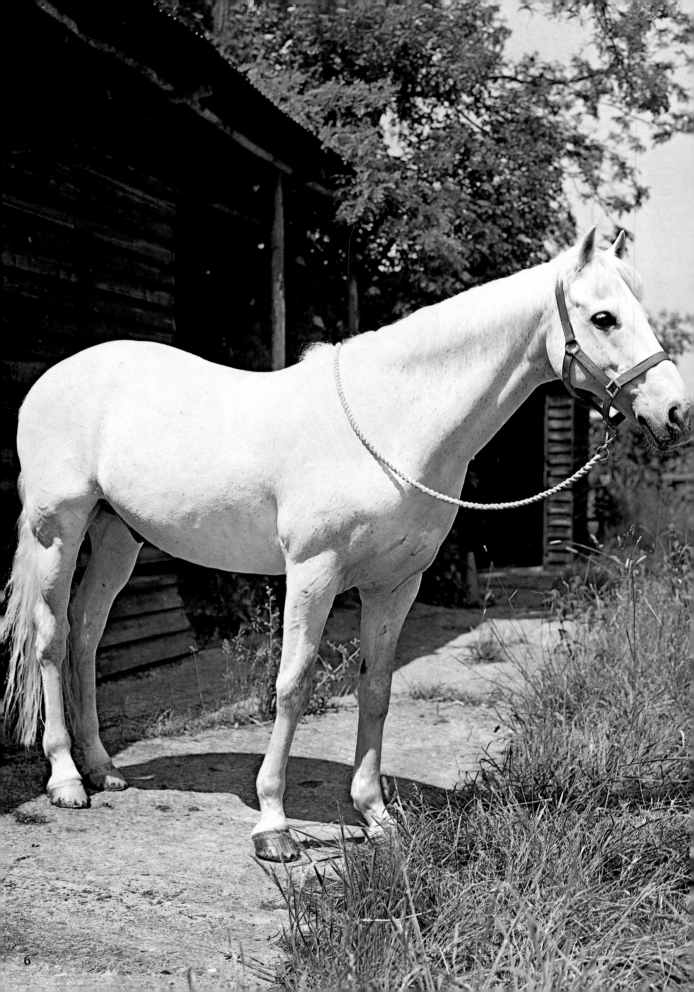

then over the centuries they became increasingly heavily armed, protected by coats of armour and carried by huge chargers that themselves wore heavy armour. This combination of heavy armour and charger was pre-eminent during the Middle Ages, and although later the pendulum swung back towards lighter horses and arms, the cavalry continued to influence the destinies of nations until the invention of firearms restored the power of the infantry and displaced the horse altogether from the battlefield. Now cavalry has no place in modern warfare, but armies all over the world continue to maintain small cavalry units for ceremonial purposes, a proud reminder of the horse's three thousand years of active military service.

Top right. Mounted bandsman with drum horse of the Household Cavalry Band.

Below. KingsTroop, Royal Horse Artillery.

Horses of the Dawn

The horse is the product not only of a domesticating process five thousand years long, but also of an evolutionary process spanning some fifty million years. Its evolution began with the odd-looking 'dawn horse', *Eohippus*, which lived in Eocene forests and browsed the succulent undergrowth–grasses did not occur at that time. It was about the size of the Labrador retriever *right* and probably looked somewhat like a tapir; its unique feature was that it possessed four toes on the front limb but three on the hind.

Over the course of millions of years *Eohippus* underwent various gradual changes and gave rise to more advanced ancestral horses, *Mesohippus* and *Miohippus;* each had three toes on the forefoot as well as three on the hind. By the Miocene epoch, about twenty-five million years later, the fossil record shows that the horse was about midway in its evolution, both in form and in geological time. From *Miohippus* there evolved two separate branches of the

horse family; one eventually became extinct, but from the other came the true horses. The more advanced of these was *Merychippus:* it was taller, with longer limbs built for sustained running. It still had three toes on each foot but the outer ones were much reduced so that it walked on tiptoe. At this time a rich new food source had appeared on the plains–grass. *Merychippus* had developed long durable teeth for taking advantage of this.

The descendants of *Merychippus* divided into six lines. The most important of these was *Pliohippus,* the first truly one-toed horse. Finally, about one million years ago, at the end of the Pliocene epoch, there gradually came about the transition from *Pliohippus* to *Equus,* the genus to which all modern horses belong, including the zebras, onagers and asses.

Wild Horses

All domesticated horses, whatever their breed, belong to the same species, and all are descended from the Eurasian wild horse. However, there were three subspecies of this wild horse, which gave rise to different domestic types, the so-called 'hot-blooded' and 'cold-blooded' breeds.

Wild horses of all three subspecies occurred in prehistoric times in immense numbers. Prehistoric man slaughtered them for food, and accumulated huge piles of their bones near his cave dwellings. Historic man went on killing wild horses because they raided crops or competed with his herds for pasture. Today only a few hundred survive in the wild, on the borders of the great Gobi Desert. This is the subspecies known as the Mongolian or Przewalski's horse. It is a sturdy dun-coloured to bay pony with erect mane and mealy muzzle. From it and another subspecies, the Steppe Tarpan, are thought to have descended all the hot-blooded breeds of domestic horses, including the Arabian and the Barb.

A second subspecies of wild horse survived in Eastern Europe until very

Left. Fortunately the Mongolian wild horse has been rescued from total extinction; breeding herds are well established in wildlife parks.

Some ancient domesticated pony breeds such as the Exmoor and the German Dülmen *right* still retain the characteristic mealy muzzle of the Mongolian wild horse.

recently. This was the Steppe Tarpan, a dark grey horse with black eel-stripe down the spine. Together with the Mongolian wild horse it was the progenitor of all present-day light-weight or riding breeds. The last wild Tarpan was killed in 1879, but it had interbred with domestic ponies, and several attempts were made by experimental breeders in Poland and at Munich Zoo to re-establish the breed by rounding up all ponies that resembled the Tarpan and breeding selectively from them. The resulting horse if not a true Tarpan, bears a striking similarity to it, with its dorsal stripe and black mane and tail.

Top left. A Tarpan stallion showing flehmen—making a characteristic scent-savouring face.

Centre top. A Tarpan grooms his flank. The starling is hunting insects flushed by the horse's hoofs.

Bottom left. A pair of Tarpan graze peacefully together.

Top right. Two stallions show peaceful intent by grooming one another.

Bottom right. Ears back, the warning signal of equine aggression.

Heavy Horses

The third subspecies of wild horse was the Forest Tarpan. Only in eastern Europe did it survive the Middle Ages. All forest animals tend to be bigger than their relatives of the open, and the Forest Tarpan was taller than the Steppe Tarpan. It looked much like the modern Norwegian Dun, and from it were bred the famous Great Horse and the heavy draught breeds of northern Europe. These horses were known as 'cold-blooded', to distinguish their type from the 'hot-blooded' descendants of the other two races. ('Hot' and 'cold' have nothing to do with actual blood temperature, but refer to temperament, the light horses being active and fiery, the great horses more passive.)

Top left. Brewers still use dray horses as an economical and decorative means of transport in cities.

Right and bottom left. Heavy horses are no longer indispensable on the modern farm but are still spectacular at agricultural shows.

Oriental Breeds

The most ancient of all hot-blooded breeds is the Arabian horse, whose history can be traced to Old Testament times. It is the foundation of all the other noble Oriental breeds, including the Barbary horse, or Barb. The Romans never knew of the existence of the Arab or the Barb; Europeans only discovered them during the crusades of the twelfth and thirteenth centuries. Then, they were so impressed with their speed and elegance that they brought home large numbers to England, Spain and France. Here the Orientals interbred with and improved the native horses, producing the many excellent breeds of light horse which we have today.

Left. The fine black Barbs of the Hausa horseman of Northern Nigeria are extraordinarily hardy and swift with characteristic convex profile.
Top right. The donkey is a serviceable mount for the Hausa boy fetching water, but lacks the speed and prestige of its distant relative the Barb.
Bottom right. The Emir of Kano enthroned on a splendidly caparisoned Barb.
Below. An Arabian grey, showing characteristic concave profile. Many modern pure-bred Arabians are grey.

Many native pony breeds used to resemble the wild horse in colour, being most usually dun or bay. But an infusion of Arab blood not only refines their conformation, producing a more tapering head and a prouder carriage, it gives the coat a silky texture and introduces exotic colouring. The coat of a horse does not by itself identify a breed, but in some breeds the colour is an important and necessary feature. A grey coat is one made up of white hairs on a dark skin, and breeds such as the Camargue, Lippizaner and Percheron are always grey. Palamino, on the other hand, is a colour, not yet a breed. A Palamino horse may be any size, but its coat should be light chestnut or the colour of a newly-minted gold coin, with white mane and tail. Arabians themselves are often Palaminos, as are Connemara, Hafflinger and Welsh ponies.

Left. Certain breeds of grey horses such as the Lippizaner and the Camargue are always born brown or even black, and do not moult to the light adult grey until four years old or more.

Right. In Europe Palamino ponies are a colour, not a breed. In North America a Palamino breed is being established.

Native Ponies

Centuries of spartan subsistence in rugged country have left their mark on British native ponies. These are often of ancient lineage, descendants of the Celtic pony used for pack and chariot by the early inhabitants of these islands. Many breeds run semi-wild on some of the most barren and exposed tracts of mountain and moorland in the country, with little shelter and very sparse grazing. They are therefore extremely hardy and tough, and very surefooted on the roughest ground.

Left. The Highland Pony is the biggest and strongest of all the British moorland ponies and is capable of carrying a mature stag over rough and boggy ground. It is usually dun-coloured, with dorsal stripe and black points testifying to its ancient origins. However, the Highland pony has been crossed with Arab blood to produce a lighter type of horse such as this palamino mare with her chestnut foal.

Right top. The Fell is the mountain pony of Westmorland and Cumberland, a descendant of the Celtic pony. It is strong and hardy, with an abundance of fine silky hair on its legs and jaw.

Right, centre and bottom. The Shetland is the smallest horse in the world and the most famous British pony. Native of the islands of Orkney and Shetland, off the north coast of Scotland, it is outstandingly tough, stunted by minimal grazing and hostile climate. Even with better grazing it must not grow taller than 42 inches at the withers; taller than this it loses the characteristics of the breed; very tiny Shetland ponies have been bred but these are useless animals except as pets. The most common colours are black, brown and bay, but Shetlands may be any colour–grey, dun, chestnut, strawberry roan even piebald or skewbald.

Other famous British moorland and mountain ponies are the related Exmoor and Dartmoor, the Connemara, and the Welsh. The Welsh pony is the most beautiful, due to the strong influence of Oriental blood. It combines the proud carriage of the Arab horse with the sturdiness of the mountain pony. The Exmoor is the oldest of our native breeds, with distinctive mealy muzzle like that of its wild ancestors. The Connemara is Ireland's only native pony, and another breed of great antiquity.

23

Ponies are not altogether just a smaller version of the horse. They have a very definite character of their own, and individualist personalities. The typical pony has short trim ears on a neat head, with large well-set eyes and a fine muzzle. This gives him a particularly alert and intelligent expression. Even among carefully bred show ponies, which may look very different from the original native stock, the essential pony character is all important. Centuries of fending for themselves in a harsh environment have shaped this character, and made ponies tougher than many horse breeds; it has increased their stamina and sure-footedness, while giving them a steadiness and an ability to get themselves out of trouble which make then ideal mounts for children.

Left top. Rough coated and tough, no amount of grooming will turn this weatherproof pony into a show animal; but he is willing, dependable and fun, and a great character.
Left bottom. Beautifully turned out show ponies compete in an event for matched pairs.
Right. Preparing a pony for show is hard work. Thin skinned breeds show more resentment at being groomed with a stiff brush, and many horses dislike being touched around the head and ears, and under the belly.

Summertime

Left. Horses grazing in the cool of the evening. Horses show preference for certain herd mates and will usually graze and rest with them.

Top right. During summer days horses are troubled by swarms of flies, some biting and blood-sucking, some that lay eggs under the skin, but most that are simply annoying, and tickle as they walk over the sensitive skin of the muzzle and cluster around the eyes to drink. By shaking its head a horse disperses the flies but only briefly; they soon settle again, as irritating as before.

Bottom right. The answer to the problem of tickling flies lies in co-operation. Horses stand nose-to-tail so that each benefits from the fly-swatting action of the other's tail in keeping the face free of the pests.

Foals

The natural time of the year for wild and feral horses to produce their foals is early summer when the new season's grasses are at their most nutritious, providing maximum nourishment for the nursing mare. The suckling foal will also start to nibble the grass at the age of five to ten days. Young foals are innately curious about their surroundings, and investigate anything new by circling round to look at it from all sides and sniff it. They will also pick up small unfamiliar objects in the mouth to chew them, and spit them out again. Young horses play a great deal, bucking and running by themselves or racing around with playmates of their own age, increasing muscle-power and locomotive skills and establishing social patterns. Young horses stabled on their own will kick and bite at the door or walls as a form of play, or try to stamp on their own tails. Some will kick at a wooden wall for hours, apparently just for the satisfaction of hearing the noise it makes.

The grass is always greener on the
other side of the fence.

Water Horses

In the summer, horses appear to enjoy the water much as we do: they delight in splashing along the edge of the sea or paddling in a stream to cool their feet; they will wallow and roll in water, and take long quenching sucks in thirsty weather.

Legend and myth have often connected horses with water or the sea, and ancient sculptures show horses rising from the waves. The association of the horse with the sea is well founded, for invaders and colonisers came by ship and swam their horses ashore.

At one time most of Europe was either heavily forested or partly under water, and native horse breeds survive in a few of the watery places still left undrained to the present time. Most famous of these is the grey Camargue pony, which together with the famous black cattle of the region, roams the inhospitable marshes of the Rhône delta in semi-wild herds.

Sleeping Horses

Unlike cattle and other grazing animals that appear to need little or no sleep, horses may sleep for up to seven hours in the twenty-four, mostly during the hottest time of the day. They do not have regular patterns of resting or sleeping, and the length of time spent asleep seems to vary not only according to the breed but also depending on hunger and comfort. Most horses doze standing up, but will also stretch out full length on the ground, especially in the spring and autumn to expose the body to warmth from the sun. Foals, like all baby animals, need to sleep very much more than do adults; for it is during sleep that most of a baby animal's growing takes place. A foal will lie down while its mother continues to graze; gradually its head nods as it dozes off, until it finally stretches out full length along the ground as it falls into deep sleep. The mare may doze while her foal sleeps, but always remains alert enough to leap to its defence or shepherd it out of danger should any threaten.

Overleaf. A grey, chestnuts and bays roaming free in the summer *left*, and two carthorses *right*, turned out for the winter.

Winter

The horse's summer coat is sleek and silky, but in the autumn a heavier coat is grown in preparation for the winter. Ponies that rough it outside in northern winters where it is nearly always unpleasantly wet as well as cold, need all the protection they can get from their shaggy double coats and profuse manes and tails. Temperature has been a chief moulder of horse types. Cold northern climates and mountainous regions have produced stocky thick-coated animals, while hot climates produced noble, elegant horses with fine coats.

Left and bottom right. Ponies nearest the ancestral wild horse pattern are best fitted to survive bleak northern winters.

Top right. Riding horses with aristocratic blood and fine coats cannot winter outdoors. They must be stabled in the warm, but enjoy exercise in the snow.

The Working Horse

Ploughing is a labour once carried out entirely with the help of draught animals, but today the tractor has taken over this onerous task on large farms throughout most of the world. It is the small farmer and peasant who still relies on his horse for this sort of work. Its versatility is irreplaceable, for what single piece of machinery can help fetch and carry, transport, plough, reap and thresh and enrich the soil for upwards of twenty years and demand so little maintenance? A really big breed such as Shire or Percheron can pull five tons, and in many countries where heavy horses have traditionally been used they are still preferred to mechanical equipment in rough, remote or mountainous regions. However, there is one area of human activity where thousands of horses used to be employed but today machines have taken over almost entirely: pit ponies, once vital to the coal-mining industry, are no longer employed underground.

Left. Ploughing with a pair of huge Shire horses requires skilled craftsmanship.

Top right. The descendants of the medieval Great Horse, almost as richly caparisoned as a ceremonial charger, here wait to take part in a ploughing championship.

Bottom right. A peasant farmer with his indispensable work-mate.

The Thoroughbred

The Arabs regarded their horse as the masterpiece of creation. It has a very distinctive appearance: a small head with concave profile, large eyes and sensitive nostrils; a short back, slender legs and small rounded hoofs. It moves easily and gracefully, with proud carriage and tail carried high.

The Arabian has been crossed with other breeds to produce very fast horses with great powers of endurance. The swiftest of all these is the British Thoroughbred, which English and Irish breeders consider to be a better-made animal than the Arabian. In size, speed, jumping ability, deportment and symmetry it far exceeds its progenitor, yet still retains that horse's fire and courage; and it is about as fast as it is mechanically possible for an animal to be that is also capable of carrying a man on its back.

The Thoroughbred is regarded as the ideal cross to produce hunters and show jumpers. The hunter is a type, and varies according to the country being hunted over. In the English Midlands a near Thoroughbred is needed to gallop over grasslands and take the strongly fenced pastures in its stride; whereas such a horse would be at a disadvantage trying to pick his way up and down stony moorland coombes. Here a strong compact little horse is ideal, a first or second cross between a Thoroughbred and a native pony.

The Irish have been breeding hunters for several centuries by crossing the Thoroughbred with the Connemara pony or the Irish Draught horse to produce big, courageous and surefooted animals, with an inbred jumping ability and staying power. Quite a number of international show jumpers are of the Irish hunter type.

Hunting and horse-racing have been part of the sporting scene for centuries, but a fairly new sport which has evolved out of these and other exhibitions of horsemanship is three-day eventing. This calls for a horse of unusual all-round ability. There are five distinct phases in eventing: dressage, road and tracks, steeplechasing, cross-country and show-jumping. Each involves different paces and different abilities, and both horse and rider must be equally at home and trained in all phases.

Spanish Horses

The Andalusian horse was the most famous breed in Europe until the creation of the Thoroughbred. It was founded by Oriental horses brought by the invading Moors in the eighth century; these crossed with the native Spanish ponies, at that time little changed from the indigenous wild horse. In the Middle Ages the Andalusian was in demand all over Europe as a cavalry and parade horse, and was trained to perform various tricks during battles to frighten the enemy infantry. This breed has contributed to the establishment of other famous breeds such as the Lippizaner, the horse closely associated with the Spanish Riding School in Vienna. Lippizaner stallions are the best-trained horses in the world; many of their displays are still based on the medieval cavalry exercises.

Top left. The *Capriole* is the peak of training. The horse half rears, then leaps off his hind legs. At the top of his leap he kicks his hind legs out in a straight line making a beautiful momentary picture.

Bottom left. However highly-trained a horse, he is not required to learn movements foreign to his nature. The rear is a natural stance employed by fighting stallions.

Right. Lunging on a long line is part of a horse's basic training. It is used to strengthen a young animal, and supple and relax the schooled horse.

54

Driving

Driving has been a sport as well as a means of transport since the beginning of historic times. Greek and Roman charioteers were perhaps the earliest to harness several horses together and drive them as fast as possible. In the eighteenth century, driving a coach and four became a very fashionable pastime in Europe, and today in almost every part of the world driving is still a sport and recreation. Horses have an innate fear of being followed. A driving horse must be taught to overcome any fear of whatever carriage, coach or gig he is harnessed to. As well as being schooled to obey signals of command, a fully-trained horse will also automatically allow room for the carriage when turning through a gate.

The Wild West

The original prehistoric home of the ancestral horse was the plains of North America. From there wild horses spread from continent to continent by crossing ice and land bridges which existed in those days. Then, inexplicably, the horse disappeared from the entire North American continent; why it should have become extinct there while flourishing in Europe and Asia is a total mystery. Nonetheless, the American prairies remained ungrazed by horses until these were reintroduced by colonists in the sixteenth century. Then it was not long before the imported horses escaped and ran wild; by the end of the next century the American prairies were once again grazed by herds of horses, from Mexico to the Canadian border. But soon the wild

Top left and right. The rodeo was originally a round-up of cattle but is now a special show where cowboys give exhibitions of their skills.

Bottom left. Fording the Rio Grande.

mustang was being caught again and turned into the invaluable cow-pony, from which eventually was bred the Quarter horse, the oldest breed in America, named for its speed over the short quarter-mile race tracks of the period.

Bottom right. Indian family in Monument Valley, Arizona. In a very short time after the reintroduction of the horse to North America Indian tribes acquired them, usually by raids, and became superb horsemen.

Australia

Australia was also a continent without horses until the seventeenth century. Its best-known breed today is the Waler, a mixture of many breeds, and named after the state of New South Wales, which has ideal horse breeding country. As in North America and many other parts of the world horses escaped and ran wild; in Australia they are known as Brumbies and are said to be almost uncatchable in their rock-strewn scrubland home, and so wild as to be untameable if eventually caught.

Left and top right. Stockmen tend cattle in New South Wales.

Instincts

However domesticated the horse may be after thousands of years' association with man, patterns of wild behaviour still persist. Stallions fight by lashing out at each other with the hind feet or trying to bite neck and withers. *Top left.* Only stallions of equal rank will fight; a subordinate horse flees from a dominant horse.

When two horses meet for the first time they circle one another a short distance apart before touching nostrils, then each horse investigates the other's tail and body with the tip of its nose. If they decide to be friendly, they nibble each other's neck. *Bottom left.*

Grazing horses *right* seldom take more than one or two mouthfuls before moving a step, and two animals, even ones that are friends, usually graze well apart.

New Forest Ponies

Ponies were running wild in England's New Forest in the eleventh century, in the reigns of King Canute and William the Conqueror; and some two thousand or more still roam the Forest. Today a new motorway bisects what was once the Forest of the Royal Hunt, and the thundering din of heavy traffic reverberates through the glades. Yet the ponies have adapted to this new invasion as they have adapted to previous activities of man over the centuries, and continue their peaceful and unfettered forest lives to the delight of anyone who has the time to pause and follow them. They are as much part of our heritage as the deer and other elusive wild life that share the Forest, and a colourful and fascinating reminder of our historic and prehistoric past.

INDEX

Where possible the horses are identified by breed or activity e.g. Arab, carriage. Otherwise the horses are indexed under their various colours.